Grow Rich *with* Assets

Fill your life with passion, excitement, energy, and purpose.

My personal stories of success and failure in business and commercial real estate.

Written by
KEVIN ERWIN
Edited by Cheryl LePlatt

ISBN: 1477686290
ISBN 13: 9781477686294

Table of Contents

Foreword

This is a book about my adventure through life, many examples of success and some of failure. I would not consider myself a writer and definitely do not have any experience writing. This book consists of my thoughts and personal opinions on what it takes to be successful. The book includes several personal experiences in my life in business and in real estate.

I hope this book can help you on your journey to success as you build confidence in the fact that anyone can be successful if he or she has passion and determination. My personal experiences will help you avoid the pitfalls on your journey.

I am writing this book from memory, and the points I make are my personal opinions. Do not make investing, building, or permitting decisions based solely on my advice or opinions.

Part 1:
The Assets Pay My Bills

How to become wealthy

For most people, becoming wealthy means getting a good education and then finding a good job. It is amazing how the public school system, as well as colleges and universities, constantly talk about your educational goals and how your education will eventually help you obtain that great job. I usually tell people, especially younger people, that they do not want a job; they obviously look at me in a weird way when I make that statement.

The fact is that few wealthy people actually have a job. I am not saying they do not work. The wealthy work for themselves; they do not work for somebody else. The wealthy normally work harder than people with jobs. The goal is to eventually own as many assets as you can. Assets are what generate income and create your cash flow.

What are assets? They can include many different things. The most common types of assets include businesses, properties, or royalties. A business, property, or royalty can potentially create unlimited revenue for the owner.

After graduating from college (with no money), I finally found a job with a small auto parts distribution company outside of Detroit. I was happy to get the job since I now had a few dollars in my pocket. One year later I realized that I would continue to have those few dollars in my pocket if I remained at this job. Looking back now, I am happy that the owner refused to increase my salary. If my salary had slowly increased, I might have stayed at that job and would still be financially poor today.

Take charge and be determined

I know many people who are content in their everyday 9-5 jobs, or at least they tell me that. One good example is a friend of mine who states things are going well at the job he has had for the last 10 years. He drives old cars and is always concerned about money and what things cost. Maybe he is happy in that lifestyle, but I know I would not be. I do not want to be forced to go into the office every day, and besides I like to sleep in. I would rather drive a Porsche than a 7-year-old Honda Accord.

Many people have good ideas and good intentions of starting businesses. However, many people lack the ability to take a risk so they are doomed to remain in their jobs. I believe I am of average intelligence, but what has given me the edge over many of my peers is the ability to take calculated risks. The people who will not take the next step are the "what if" people. They will say, what if this, what if that. My wife constantly said this to me during my first two business ventures.

I would just respond with, "What if the sky falls, and then we will not have to worry about anything."

The first business I started was a wedding videography business. When I first mentioned the idea of starting this business, it was as if I had asked my wife for a kidney.

All I heard from her was, "We can't do that."

I pushed forward, and within two years we were booking over 40 weddings per year. My wife was very good at wedding videography but would never have had the chance to own her own business if we had not taken the risk to start this business.

Risk is often associated with something bad. To me the word corresponds more closely to courage and strength. I am obviously not talking about the risk of betting on a horse at the track. When you have done your homework on a business you want to start and you know in the back of your mind it will be successful, you need to push forward and make it happen.

Did you join the rat race?

You are a member of the rat race if you or your family continues to purchase bigger homes and nicer cars as your income increases. If your financial goals revolve around purchasing a bigger and more expensive home, you are not going down the path to financial independence. Why is it that people tend to work harder and harder to purchase larger homes, more expensive cars, in-ground pools, large gas grills, huge TV's, etc? In the process of working harder and trying to get that next promotion they are actually causing more personal stress, usually spending less time with family, and paying more income tax along the way.

I chuckle when someone states that another person is wealthy. I always ask, "How do you know?"

The response is usually something like, because the other person makes $150k per year. Remember, financial wealth is not what you earn; financial wealth is the value of the assets you currently own. We will talk more about this later.

Your home is not an asset because it does not generate positive cash flow; in fact, it only creates expense. As one purchases a larger home, the property tax, insurance, electric bill, and maintenance costs all increase. I would still recommend a house over an apartment as long as you will live there more than two years because it will, over time, increase in value. Instead of purchasing a bigger home or building the new pool, use the money from the increased value of your home to purchase an asset.

To repeat, assets include businesses, properties, or some type of royalties. This new asset will generate more cash for your everyday life. The bigger home only creates greater expenses. If you want to purchase a bigger home, that is ok; however, please do not call it an investment.

About two years ago I purchased a small strip center instead of buying a pool, a new car, or bigger house. I spent $150,000 to purchase the strip center. The strip center gave me an additional $30,000 in positive cash flow per year. An added bonus was that I was able to sell the property one year later for $185,000 more than the purchase price. I will go into greater detail later in the book on how I determine when to purchase a commercial property.

Good debt

Most people acquire bad debt through the purchase of cars, TV's, and many other items. Bad debt ruins your financial future. Good debt plays an important part in your future plans to become wealthy. When you borrow money to earn money that is good debt. When I purchased the commercial property I mentioned earlier, I borrowed $450,000 along with my $150,000 down payment to make the purchase. This property generated an extra $30,000 in yearly revenue.

Banks are more than eager to lend money to purchase property. The physical property serves as collateral for the bank. The bank knows that if the borrower defaults on the loan they can recover the money owed to them by reselling the property. The banks are not as eager to lend money for a business. If the business fails, the banks have very little recourse to recover their money. Since the business loan is less secure, the interest rate the lender charges will be higher. The business loan generally has to be paid back in a shorter time; for example, 10 years for a business loan in comparison to 20 to 30 years for a commercial property. This shorter loan payback period means a much higher monthly loan payment.

For a new entrepreneur just starting, one may want to consider a venture with relatively low cash needed to start the business. The problem with a business loan to start the business is that right from the beginning there is pressure to make money. Falling behind on loan payments from the beginning will surely mean failure. Using the internet to start a business is a relatively low cost way to start a business. If the internet business fails, your personal finances are not ruined also.

Cash flow

I personally stopped working when my assets earned enough money so I did not have to work. My neighbor asked me several times if I won the lottery. This neighbor could not understand how I still paid my bills but did not work at a formal job. The neighbor did not see past the idea of working to pay the bills. She and many others do not understand the power of purchasing assets to pay your bills so you do not have to work a normal job. I would rather have my assets earn me money than have to get up early each morning for work. My cash flow primarily comes from commercial property investments. My commercial properties continue to pay me day in and day out.

I have gone months without visiting a property or talking to any tenants. Sometimes I get bored, so I just take a drive to look at a property. Sometimes there is work to be done at a property. Finding a new tenant is what takes the most time, but that does not happen that often.

Usually the work that needs to be done at a property is small in nature. Replacing sprinkler heads, a/c repair, and broken ceiling tiles are examples of common repairs. When something does need to be repaired, I rush to my phone and call the handyman or whichever contractor is right for the job. You guessed it. I do very few of the repairs myself. I decided a long time ago to focus on the things I do well, which are not many, and fixing things is not one of my strong suits. Remember, you can always find somebody to pay to do any job.

Making decisions

Life is filled with so many choices on a daily basis. There are many more psychiatrists in the United States than in Russia. The reason is that in the United States people have to make countless more decisions on a daily basis, and some people become overwhelmed. It is easier to go to your job every day and perform the same task day in and day out. This lifestyle is less stressful but definitely more boring.

Being an entrepreneur requires numerous decisions on a daily basis. This is why the entrepreneur or president of a company makes so much money. Making many decisions can be daunting at times even for the seasoned entrepreneur. My solution is to gather all the information I need within two days, sit down at the dinner table, and give myself one hour to come up with a decision. Do not allow yourself to become bogged down with indecisiveness. This can paralyze you. Be aware you will not always make the correct decision. We are human.

Recently I painted a retail property, and it looked hideous afterwards. The green color I had selected looked good sitting on my kitchen table, but on the building it was bad news. This mistake cost me $500 to repaint using a different color. The point is, as a business owner you will be faced with making many decisions. Work hard at making the best decision. Once a decision is made, move on.

Setting up your business

Setting up your business is the easiest part of starting a business. It is also one of the most important things to do. If you operate your business as a sole proprietor or partnership, you put all of your personal assets at financial risk. For example, John Smith goes into business selling socks and sets up the business as John Smith dba Sock World. (DBA stands for Doing Business As). A person wearing one of Sock World's socks slips on her kitchen floor breaking her neck. The injured person cannot only sue Sock World; she can also sue John Smith. John Smith has now placed all of his assets in jeopardy.

Since people tend to file lawsuits more frequently in today's world, protect your personal assets. The simplest way to protect your personal assets is to set up an LLC (Limited Liability Company) or Type S Corporation. These business structures protect your personal assets from lawsuit. The annual tax returns can be put through your normal personal tax returns. This makes the tax preparation process fairly simple.

Setting up an LLC or corporation is uncomplicated. The hardest part is picking out the name. The name you choose must end with LLC if it is a Limited Liability Company. The LLC can be set up over the phone by calling the I.R.S. @ 800-829-4933 or by going online @ www.irs. gov. It literally takes about 10 minutes. Once completed you will have your Federal ID and will be able to operate your new business as an LLC or corporation.

Many states also require you to register your new business. In my state of Florida, this can be done very easily online @ Sunbiz.org. Please do not pay an attorney or CPA to set up your LLC; it is too easy to not do on your own. I paid an attorney $500 to set up my first LLC. What a waste of money. If you plan on having employees, you may want to incorporate under a subchapter S.

Set up business checking accounts, and do not use personal accounts for business affairs. If this is a home business, I would recommend purchasing a PO Box at the local post office. I would also set up a separate phone number for business calls only. I currently use Vonage for $15 a month, but Ooma is a new, cheaper option. The point is to operate your business as a business and not mix personal matters.

After I graduated from college, I was a part-time bank teller for six months. One thing I noticed about the wealthy is that they spent their money wisely. They did not pull into the parking lot in the latest BMW, and they did not wear expensive clothing. When I saw people pull into the parking lot of the bank in a luxury vehicle, I would notice as I processed their transactions that there was not much money in their account. As the saying goes, "these people wore a big hat, but did not have any cattle". They pretended they were wealthy to "keep up with Joneses" but really were poor financially. This type of behavior eventually catches up to you and the more big hats you own, the less chance you will have of financial freedom in the future.

During the 1990s I played in a men's golf league each week, and often I would see a short guy, all dirty and with a beard, doing miscellaneous work around the golf course. His name was Al. In my mind Al was a worker doing odd jobs for the golf club, and my thought at the time was that I would say "hi" if he walked by. I had no interest in talking with him. Why would I want to waste my time? One day as I was walking up to the club to play golf, Al was digging some type of hole in the ground. I could only see him from the chest up since he was standing in the hole. I said "hi" as I walked by.

After paying my green fees in the clubhouse, I started talking with the assistant pro about how I wanted to start purchasing rental properties.

Since I had many questions at this point in my life and was not sure where to begin, the assistant pro said, "Let me introduce you to the owner. He owns this golf course and several other golf courses and has a huge portfolio of rental properties."

"OK, great!" I followed the assistant pro outside and over to the hole in the ground.

He pointed to the man standing in the hole and said, "This is Al, the owner of the club."

This person, the one to whom I did not want to give the time of day, was probably the richest man in town. He was not concerned about wearing big hats, but he had plenty of cattle. He gave me some good advice on purchasing rental properties. I almost missed out on this advice due to my preconceived notions that successful people drive expensive cars and wear fancy suits and certainly would not be found digging a ditch at a golf course.

Right the ship

Righting the ship can be a difficult step; it is hard for humans to change their habits. Tendencies become harder to change as we age. If you are younger and living with your parents, continue to do that. You will be able to save money more quickly since you most likely will not be spending any money on housing and possibly very little on food.

Young people like to purchase lots of clothing. This, in general, is a waste of money. People tend to wear 15 percent of their clothing 85 percent of the time. So the odds are the new piece of clothing will not make it into the 15 percent, and you will not even wear it. If you do need some clothes, purchase them at the end of their season, such as purchasing shorts at the end of the summer and long sleeve shirts in February. The prices are much cheaper.

If you think you have to purchase something, wait two days to think about it. If you are still adamant about making the purchase, consider going back to buy the item. Most of the time you will forget about the item and realize you really did not need it.

If you are married, hopefully you discussed finances before the wedding and your husband or wife is not a chronic shopper. If only one half of the marriage has a goal to become financially independent, it will never work. Both partners must have the goal of financial independence for it to work. If you have a significant other or are engaged, it does not matter how good looking he or she is, if that person spends money without a second thought, you may want to run fast in the opposite direction or endure a lifetime of being poor.

When I was first married I made $18,000 per year. My wife made $17,000 per year for a grand total of $35,000. We were able to save $450 per month while owning a small house and having two older cars. What I remember most was purchasing and eating generic brand yogurt and thinking someday I will be able to purchase Yoplait. It was not easy to save that $450 per month, but we made it happen.

What is the condition of your finances? Are you spending more than you are earning? Are you spending **a lot** more than you are earning? Or are you spending about the same that you are earning and not saving anything? Do you have **any** money saved? If you are not saving money, you **must** either spend less or earn more. It is that simple.

I will go over different ways in your everyday life that you can stop spending as much money and start saving more. I will not be advising you to stop living or enjoying things such as going to Starbucks or super-sizing your fries. Once we go through ways to reduce spending, we will talk about the building cash phase. You need some money to make money. It would be difficult to purchase a property or start a business with zero money. In the next few pages, we will talk about what you should do with the money you have accumulated while you were building your cash reserves.

Once we have some cash, what opportunities do we have to make a lot more money with that cash? We will discuss several different ideas including residential properties, commercial properties, new business start-ups, and business purchases.

Go to a local store such as Staples and purchase a spreadsheet. The spreadsheet should be used to manually input monthly expenses.

**Home Budget
2012**

	January	February	March	April	May	June	July
Expenses							
Auto Insurance	$139.90	$139.90	$139.90	$139.90			
Discover Credit Card	$579.62	$927.13	$1,515.93	$805.04			
Visa Credit Card	$2,158.49	$2,889.94	$3,656.21	$2,261.76			
Health Insurance	$256.00		$256.00				
Home Loan	$1,650.15	$1,650.15	$1,650.15	$1,650.15			
Home Phone	$26.48	$26.15	$26.51	$26.98			
Cable/internet	$107.37	$107.37	$111.92	$107.88			
Water	$60.32	$72.16	$99.92	$105.73			
Electric	$121.65	$115.30	$96.60	$125.82			
Cell Phone	$172.30	$172.21	$174.47	$174.47			
Total	$5,272.28	$6,100.31	$7,727.61	$5,397.73			

As you pay a bill, input the amount in your spreadsheet to keep it current. This will let you know what your expenses are month to month. It is important to visually see what is happening with your money. The bills should be paid online. Not only is it safer than sending snail mail, the cost of a stamp is saved. You are saving money, and your bills are still being paid. As you receive your bills, pay them right away. Why not? If you owe the money, pay it. This will also prevent any late fees especially with credit cards.

If you eventually own a commercial property, pay the contractors right away after the job is done correctly. When the contractor knows you pay your bills promptly, he will be happy to work on your project before working for someone who pays poorly.

First let's look at the common household expenses, the expenses that happen month after month. These are the expenses that need a closer examination and would include your car payment, house payment or rent, electric bill, water, phone, home insurance, auto insurance, life insurance, cable. Many things in your everyday life can cost you less if you try or make different choices.

Not having a car payment by purchasing an older car or keeping the car you have if it is paid for are ways to save money in order to build cash. Later, when you're a millionaire, you can think about the nicer car. When I was young my grandfather always told me that new cars will send you to the poor house. I did not know what a poor house was as a 10 year old, but I knew I did not want to go there. Was he right? Well, new cars may not send you to the poor house, but they will keep you poor. With a new car you will need full coverage auto insurance; your auto loan or lease will require it.

If you have a used vehicle, keep it. Cars these days last a long time. I have a 2003 Toyota Camry with

145,000 miles. Yes, I would like a new car, but the Toyota still runs good, it is paid off and requires liability only insurance. And, yes, I will need minor repairs once in a while, but that is still much cheaper in the long run that purchasing a new vehicle. If you need to purchase a used vehicle, look at the magazine, *Consumers Report,* for the vehicles they recommend. I would suggest a 5 to 10 year old Honda or Toyota; they are very reliable.

If you have a poor driving record, this is even more reason to have an older vehicle. A poor driving record with a new car equals high auto insurance. Auto insurance rates should be quoted out with other companies every three years or sooner if you feel the rates have increased excessively. I used to sell property and casualty insurance, and it was amazing how many people would stay with the same company for 10, 20, or 30 years. Many people would say, "I like my agent" after I gave them a quote. They could see their agent did not like them as much. My personal recommendation is to call Amica Mutual for auto insurance, and if you are in the military call USAA insurance.

Next let's talk about your house payment or rental payment. A house is a good investment. How often do we hear that?

My response is, "How much money did your house make you last year?"

The answer is zero. If it is a rental property, that is a different story. We will talk about rental properties later in the book. The fact is your home not only did not make you money but is actually your largest expense. Your house has many ongoing monthly expenses such as interest on the debt, property insurance, water, electric, landscaping, and repairs. Yes, we have to live somewhere, but we can choose to live in a smaller house with smaller monthly expenses.

A common trend is that as a person's income goes up he will tend to purchase more expensive houses and more expensive cars. That is called joining the rat race, as mentioned earlier. Many people cannot get out of the rat race. They are more concerned with keeping up with the neighbors and buying the latest car and best outdoor grill.

I have always asked, "Why purchase an outdoor grill when you have a stove you can turn on in two seconds?"

My wife has always felt differently about the grill.

I do not think renting is a bad idea if you can find a good deal. In the year 2012 good deals are everywhere. Many investors have purchased homes to flip only to be stuck with them as the values decreased. Investors are now purchasing foreclosed and short sale homes at great prices and are leasing them out. With the large market of rental homes, the prices look good for someone trying to rent. Remember, the cost of housing, whether it is a home purchase or rental payment, is an expense.

Many successful commercial property owners and business owners live in condos or townhomes because these offer a place to live with less cost and less maintenance.

Your electric and water bill can be reduced. There are many things in your house that consume electricity without you even realizing it. These are things you do not use or do not use very often and consist of clocks, VCR/DVD players, and computers. If you have cable, turn off the cable box after you turn off the TV. Also, not all the lights in your house have to be on all the time. Make it a habit to turn lights off. Water in general is not expensive, so I would not focus much on that. Phone expenses can be reduced quite a bit. If you have a cell phone, you may not need a home phone at all. Go with the basic plan if you still want to keep a home phone. A better option is to go with Magic Jack for $20 per year or some type of internet phone such as Vonage.

Building cash

Now that we have reduced our expenses, we need to save as much money as possible as quickly as possible. This could mean working extra hours, a second job, or maybe doing without cable until you have saved $50,000. Where do I put the money as I am saving it? Stock market, mutual funds, gold, silver, bonds, options, futures contracts, under mattress, savings – all are available options.

This money should go into a federally insured savings account. The online accounts work well, with better interest than the local neighborhood banks. I have had an account at ING Direct for years.

The main goal here is to save money to purchase an asset. An asset, **again**, is something that earns money, unlike the home you live in. Gold and silver do not earn you any money; they just sit in a safe deposit box. A bond will earn you money, but if interest rates go up, your bond is now worth less if you want to sell it. Concerning mutual funds, we hear all the time that we should invest for the long term. Investment companies say over a 10, 20, or 30 year period you are likely to earn 10, 12, or 15% per year. I wonder what 10, 20, or 30 year period they are talking about. I have had mutual funds for many decades. The value never seems to change much. My wife put 50k in an IRA about 10 years ago, and it was invested into an S&P 500 index mutual fund. The value is about the same today. I am not sold on the mantra, invest for the long term. How long is long term? I know it is too long for me.

You have now saved your 50k or whatever sum of money you set as your goal, and you have also paid down your debt (hopefully). I said hopefully paid down your debt also, because this affects your credit score. Your credit score needs to be above 700. You can go to annualcreditreport.com once a year and get your score for free. Basically, what you need to do is pay your bills on time, all the time. Do not worry about all the reasons your credit score will fluctuate. I repeat, just pay your bills on time, all the time, and your score will steadily improve.

Credit cards can earn you money. I would recommend that you have two credit cards that both
pay cash back with purchases. Cash back is the best
reward, as opposed to travel miles or some point system at a certain retailer. Cash can be used anywhere.
Do not make purchases with a credit card unless the
bill can be paid in full. If this is a problem for you, drop
down to one credit card with a $1000 balance to be
used only for emergencies.

Debit cards are not a safe way to conduct business.
If the card and password are stolen, there is no safe-
guard to protect your money from being removed
from your bank account. Also, debit cards do not give
you cash back like credit cards do. The worst thing you
can do is carry around a check book and write checks
for each transaction. Not only is this time consuming,
but if your checkbook is stolen bad checks may start
appearing all over town.

Make it happen

Making it happen comes down to you. Do you have
what it takes to operate a successful business or purchase an apartment building?

In 1995, I was working an inside sales position that
paid $18,000 per year and was going nowhere. There
was no chance of promotion or excelling in this small
business. I volunteered to do outside sales, but the
owner was not interested. I learned many things at
this business, the first being that some business owners can be flat out liars.

I was told when I started that a small portion of the company's annual earnings would be invested each year in my personal 401k plan. I understand that things change and there are no guarantees, so was not too upset when I was told after year one that this benefit was now being discontinued. Three years later, however, I found out that the other three employees continued to get contributions to their 401k plans even though I was told by the owner that the company had discontinued that benefit.

When I questioned the owner, he said, "Too bad. I am the owner and will do what I want."

Also, I was a part-time prisoner of the company. I had to arrive at 8:00 am sharp each and every day and could not leave the prison grounds until 5:00 pm. I learned very quickly that I did not want to keep working for this owner or any other company. I became very motivated at this point to become my own boss.

But what kind of company should I start or possibly purchase? That was a tough question. There are two ways to make money; you physically work and earn a certain amount per hour, this applies to salaried employees also, or you have your money work for you. I, personally, enjoy having my money work for me instead of having to be at a job every day.

Where do I put my money to work? Traditional places like savings accounts, bonds, and mutual funds will not work unless you are worth more than ten million dollars. To make it work, your money has to own assets. This could include property, businesses, a book you wrote, partial ownership in an oil well, or a right to any asset that earns money. Once this is accomplished, you will be earning money without having to personally work. This is called passive income; you don't have to actually work to earn money. I will discuss later in this book personal examples of how I accomplished this.

Currently I am earning enough passive income so I can get out of bed whenever I want. As previously mentioned, one of my neighbors used to consistently ask me if I had won the lottery because she always saw me walking my dog in the middle of the day while most people were at work. This person thinks the only way to make a living is to actually go to work. I repeatedly told my neighbor that I did not win the lottery, and I know she was always thinking, "Then how do you pay your bills?"

I just talked with someone looking to lease space to start a tobacco products business. I guess there are machines on the market a person can use in a store and actually make their own cigarettes at a deeply discounted price. I believe the person who wants to start this business is never going to be able to pull the trigger and get it going.

He talked about leasing next to another business that would help his business. Why do people think having your business next to some other particular type of business will matter when in 99.9 percent of the time it does not matter? That is not to say business location is not important. For example, opening a pawn shop in an upscale neighborhood might not be the best idea, but opening it next to a hair salon probably would not matter.

This potential tobacco business owner also wanted 500 to 600 square feet. He was not sure how to lay out the new store but wanted something nice. A business plan was something he wanted to write first. He said he had found a spot that would work but then became concerned about the plumbing in the building since the building is 50 years old. This person will never start his business because there are too many variables to which he is trying to find definite or exact answers. I will not be calling him back to lease my space because I know he will not make a decision, and I am wasting my time.

Being a landlord

My first comment is that when a contractor completes a job, and it is done correctly, pay him right away. Why not? If you owe it, pay it. Contractors remember this, and the next time you need their help they will go to your job before someone that does not pay for 40 days. You may also get a little better pricing because it is a huge hassle for contractors when they have to track down deadbeats who do not pay.

Keeping your properties maintained can give you a huge advantage over other property owners, especially owners that use management companies. These property owners tend to turn the property over to the management company and then forget about it. If they manage on their own, most do not actively keep things maintained.

I would recommend that as things break you fix them right away. If you turn a blind eye to problems, eventually your property will become run down and an eyesore. A dilapidated property is harder to rent out and makes it an easier reason for tenants to leave. Take care of your asset, and it will take care of you. And, again, why is something an asset? It is an asset because it earns you money.

The main reason to manage your commercial property yourself is because it is easy. Also, you can respond faster to tenant problems and avoid some tenants leaving over issues that can be resolved.

A common issue with a tenant is the space becoming too small; their business has grown. Sometimes you can reconfigure the space, take down a wall, add a wall, be creative, and do what it takes to keep the tenant. Many times I have had tenants move to larger spaces within the same complex or something nearby. If tenants say it's a pain to move, tell them you will pay for Two Men and a Truck to move them. If a tenant still needs to leave, be gracious and thank them for renting the space. They will see when they move to their new space how good they had it when they rented from you. They may be your tenant again in the future, so do not burn any bridges.

IT'S about the customer

Keeping your customers happy should be your first objective. Without customers or tenants there is no business. Make sure they stay happy so they will continue patronizing your business. At the title office it is the most important thing we do each day. Our customers know that if there is a question or problem regarding their closing, they can call us directly and we will solve the problem. We have Customer Appreciation parties twice per year to thank our customers for their business.

I try to keep the rental properties maintained and updated so the tenants feel they are receiving a good value for their monthly lease payment. I also give the tenants my personal cell phone number in case of an emergency. Sometimes a customer can push you or your business so far that this particular customer turns into a liability. This type of customer might be constantly calling you for irrelevant issues or consuming a large amount of your time without actually providing much income to your business. These are the customers you want to get rid of; they are doing harm to your business. So, yes, you want to take care of your customers except for the few who cause you all the grief.

Avoid getting attorneys involved in a property transaction and most other transactions. There are a small number of situations where the use of an attorney is worthwhile. Attorneys will end up dragging out the transaction by bringing up potential possibilities or hazards that will never happen or even if they do would not be a big deal. You will also become poor very quickly with the use of an attorney. They bill per hour, and the clock runs whether they are speaking to you or anyone else concerning your case. Just use common sense instead of an attorney.

There was a small commercial property I was interested in when I lived in Michigan. At the time I was fresh out of college and basically knew nothing about purchasing commercial properties. The realtor told me since it's a commercial property I had to hire an attorney, so I did. At the meeting between the real estate agent, attorney, and me, the attorney proclaimed we had a big problem. The attorney thought that a concrete wall at the back of the property was partially on the property we were looking to purchase and partially on someone else's property. At the time this seemed like a big issue and resulted in me not pursuing the property further.

Looking back now, I realize the concrete wall would not have been an issue. The wall had been there for at least 10 years, and no one cared whose property it was technically on. If it were to ever become an issue, someone could just remove it. It would have been cheap to remove the wall. The attorney cost me $500 for a 30 minute meeting.

Permits

First of all, I always intend to follow all government rules. I pay, on time, my property taxes and all the other government fees that I am assessed. There are times when the local government gets so ridiculous with the permits that it may be advantageous to consider doing a job without the permit. Some of the times to consider avoiding permits would include: replacing electrical outlets, removing small walls, flooring, minor plumbing, and fences.

Recently at an office building, I was required by the city to install not only one but two drinking fountains. Why two? One for the handicapped and one for the standing people even though the drinking fountain for the handicapped was only two inches lower than the other fountain. Why the government requires even one fountain is ridiculous. No one uses them. Water is not hard to come by; if someone needs water that urgently it would not be a problem to find water. There was a sink with running water 10 feet away.

I even asked the inspector, "Why two fountains?"

He said it was so the standing people would not have to bend over too far. So I spent $2,500 for the two useless drinking fountains.

At the final inspection for the drinking fountains, the inspector told me that I needed tempered water in the office. He said tempered water was between 85 and 110 degrees. Another permit. I had to run an electric line to the insta hot box. Another permit. The electric lines were put in along with the insta hot, but the inspector kept rejecting the work. Of course I had to pay a fee each time they came back to re-inspect, and they would not give a time so I could meet them for the inspection.

I finally found out the reason for the rejections. I had removed all of the ceiling tiles going across the ceiling so the new electric line could be viewed by the inspector. I had not removed one tile in the corner, so the inspector was unable to see two feet of the electric line. This was the reason for the multiple rejections. There was even a ladder in the corner if the inspector felt that he really needed to take a look above the one ceiling tile.

These are some of the reasons property investors at times avoid getting permits. The cities and counties should be working with you to grow your business, but it seems they turn into your enemy and fight against you getting things done for the good of your business and the community. There are a couple communities near my residence where I would think twice about purchasing a property due to the cumbersome government interference.

Play poker

When you play poker you want to give your opponents as little information as possible. You want to be as straight faced as possible so they have no idea how good a hand you have. It is many times the same in a business transaction. Do not give out unneeded information.

For example, if you are trying to purchase a mortgage company and the property it sits on for $500,000 and you believe the property alone is worth $500,000, you are not obligated to give the owner any indication of your thoughts of what the property is worth. Do not lie, be straight forward and discuss the deal

I just spoke with a friend and told him I was writing a book.

His first words were, "I could never write a book."

The fact is almost anyone can write a book. However, if you have the mindset that you cannot succeed at writing a book or doing anything else in life, guess what your results will be. I do not have any background or experience in writing a book, but I have the determination and positive attitude to get it done. Really, what is a book but just a bunch of words strung together?

as a business person, with courtesy. Nonetheless, do not let everyone know the hand you are playing.

Many times over the years real estate brokers have asked me how much cash I have to put down on a property or business that I want to purchase. The broker is calculating in his mind whether or not I actually have enough money to purchase the property or business. The broker does not want to waste his or her time. I try to answer vaguely because if they think I am light in the liquid assets (money) department they may not want to help me. Many times over the years I have been light on the money. The broker does not need to know that information, and there have been many times when I did not have enough cash to purchase an asset but still found a way to make the deal happen with creative financing or bringing in a minority partner.

10 year rule

Many people believe that it takes ten years of hard work or practice in your field to become highly successful. I believe it takes about five years of constant learning and improving with whatever you are doing to be a master at your skill. This does not mean that after five years you do not continue to learn. At the five year mark you will be knowledgeable enough to give a presentation to an auditorium of people wanting to gain knowledge of your expertise.

For example, when my wife and I started the wedding video business, we literally did not even know how to focus the camera correctly. Several years later we could explain the minute details of a video camera. We learned as the business progressed.

Stress

Stress can rob your passion and determination to reach your goals. As we become busier and more successful, many people forget to take care of themselves. If you forget to exercise and eat properly, stress will eventually start appearing in your life. Nobody can continue to perform at his highest level if too much stress is present in his or her life.

Take the time to set a normal schedule for exercising. Walking is not going to cut it. You can run, play tennis, racquetball or some other activity where you are making your heart work to 75% of capacity. For me, I run three times per week and my goal is to have my heart rate between 140 and 150 beats per minute for 20 minutes. Your body will operate more efficiently with a normal exercise regimen. Eating properly is also important; common sense is the best strategy.

Act your part

Have you ever heard someone say, "I am not a good speaker" or "I am not good at socializing at parties" or just about any topic you want to mention? What I would say is "act the part". Pretend you are good at speaking, pretend you are good at socializing, and you will eventually not need to pretend. Practicing whatever you want to be good at is the surest way to become an expert. When I first started teaching at Baker College, I am sure I was not that good an instructor, but I pretended I was. The more practice I got with each lecture, the better I became.

Attitude

Surround yourself with people who have a positive attitude. People with a bad attitude will bring you down. If you own your own business, you know that one bad apple (bad attitude) can spoil the rest. Your office and your life will become infected with negativity. People with a positive attitude will also help keep you uplifted and positive.

For example, when I was growing up every time I came up with a new business idea, which was often, my family told me very quickly that the idea was dumb, or it would not work, or you can't do that. Before long I stopped telling my family my ideas because I became tired of the negative attitude towards them. The negativity was bringing me down. What my family should have done was try to give me positive feedback along with some negative feedback. They should have told me to keep the good ideas coming.

For those dating and looking for a future wife or husband, yes, the looks are important, but a positive attitude will last a lifetime. *Being able to cook is important also.*

Fail to complete

Do you have the ability to follow through on a task until completion? Most people do not. An example of this is New Year's resolutions. They usually last one or two weeks. Look back over the last couple years of your life. What goals have you made for yourself and then followed through to accomplish? I am not talking about the goal of getting five punches at the pizza shop so you can get a free pizza. I am talking about goals that positively affect your life moving forward. To be successful you have to have the attitude that you will see a goal to the end.

Try your best, that's all you can do

One of the mottos I tell myself and others is to just do your best. In everyday life we all face situations of uncertainty or situations that are stressful.

Every morning I drive my daughter to school. As she is getting out the car I say, "Have a great day and do your best."

I want her to know that doing her best is more important to me than getting a letter grade of A or B. I also know that someone who consistently does his best, whether it is at school, on the job, or in a new business, is the type of person who will be successful.

If I am consistently trying my best, I am moving myself, my family, and my business in the right direction. I also try to improve on things on a daily, weekly, or yearly basis. The properties I own and manage are a good example. They are in constant need of repairs. My thoughts are not only to keep them managed and maintained well, but to slowly, over time, continue to improve each property. This may entail such things as improving the landscaping, painting, or just picking up some trash in back. It is not a coincidence or luck that my properties stay 100% occupied.

Get a good deal/asset value

The value of a property or business is mostly determined by your experience and doing a thorough investigation. Many real estate investors look primarily at the income the property generates. In my opinion that is a small part of the story on why or why not a particular property would be a good investment.

Some examples: Let's say the property is bringing in good cash flow relative to price, but Blockbuster rents 75% of the total space and is paying rents that are 50% above the going rate in the area. Also, Blockbuster may go out of business. So I would not look favorably on this investment due to the future outlook even though the current numbers look good.

The other end of the spectrum is a property with poor cash flow relative to price. On paper this may look like a terrible deal. This property is currently 60% vacant, and the tenants who are leasing space pay

50% less than the current market rents. However, this property is on a main road in a growing part of town. This is the type of property I look for. The future potential for this type of property is excellent. The value of the property can be increased very quickly over a short period of time. Once the value is increased, you can refinance to pull money out of the property tax free. Then what? You guessed it. This money will be used for the next property investment.

Sometimes it can be difficult to finance these types of properties because the banks also loan money on cash flow even if I try to show them the future potential of the property. When the bank is reluctant to finance a property due to poor cash flow relative to price, you will most likely have to put more cash down to do the deal. If you have no more cash, you may have to bring in a minority partner. Make sure the partner is a minority partner so you maintain control of the business. You keep control by having a least 51% ownership.

Once you gain experience and have a track record that you **pay your bills on time, all the time,** the lender will start becoming more flexible on the terms of the loan and ultimately help you get more deals done faster.

This is where you turn into a detective. Gather all the information you can get your hands on to make the most informed decisions you can.

I had a friend a few years back who was looking to purchase an office building that would be good for two tenants. He had already negotiated a price with the seller and was working with a contractor to reno-vate the property. This was during his due diligence period. My friend knew I purchased and sold commer-cial property so he asked me to stop by to give him my assessment. The property was in poor condition, inside and out, but that was not what I was concerned about. I told my friend to come out to the parking lot with me and to look around.

I then asked him, "What do you see?"

He looked around, and said, "Wow."

What he was looking at was a run down, dead part of town. There were no cars driving by. There were some neglected and vacant houses and two empty lots for sale next door.

I said, "Would you want to rent space here to run your business?"

He said, "Probably not."

I asked if he had called the realtors regarding the two vacant lots that were for sale. When he said no, I told him I had called from my car a few minutes ago. The lots had been for sale for three years, and the real-tor told me to make any offer if I was interested. This part of town was older, dilapidated, depressed, and not improving anytime soon.

I told my friend that I hoped he was not upset with my comments. He had asked for my opinion, and I thought it was only fair that I give it to him free of sugar coating. I said if this area was in the path of new development, even if ten years down the road, or if on a major road in at least an average part of town, I would say go for it. My friend had fallen in love with this property. Big mistake. After being shocked by my comments, he eventually cancelled the contract and did not purchase the property.

Listening

(so you will not get ripped off in the future)

Becoming more knowledgeable and understanding how something works or learning about new changes in your business is accomplished primarily through listening.

Recently I had to call the septic company because the distribution box collapsed, and sewage was running out into the back of the property. The point here is that I made sure to listen in order to learn as much as possible about septic systems and try to make sure I was not being ripped off. The quote for repair was $1950.00. Shocking. Fortunately for me, I have worked with this septic company for a while and through my past experience of listening to septic contractors, I knew this was a fair deal.

I have a black book of contact info that lists recommended contractors for just about any job that needs to be done. I also have a list of contractors to stay away from. I will write notes under each contractor to explain why I should or should not work with this company in the future. I am basically writing myself a note for the future.

No excuses!

We all have issues. That is not a good enough reason!

Everyone has excuses of why they do not want to do something. I am too busy, I have a cold, now is not a good time, I am too tired, I hurt my shoulder playing tennis, we are going on vacation, right now I am judgment proof, and so many more excuses I could write a book about it.

The fact is everyone is living life with the many challenges and issues that life presents. If we wait for that perfect time when the stars are aligned, we will not take action. There will always be reasons why you should not pursue your dreams. The successful person just pushes forward and makes it happen. To the successful person, it does not matter if he has a cold, hurt his shoulder, is tired, or is planning a vacation. We are only alive about 25,000 days on average, so you should make the most of the life God gave you.

I have heard the phrase, "I am judgment proof right now" several times lately. Basically, what this means is that I have no money and I will not be sued because I have no money. It is better not to be judgment proof. That means you have some level of wealth. Many lawyer friends of mine are afraid of lawsuits, which is understandable because of their field of work. There are no guarantees against a lawsuit, but being afraid of a lawsuit is no way to live your life.

Lawsuits are minimized by doing things correctly: setting up LLC's or incorporating, proper liability insurance, maintaining properties, and using sound practices in the operation of a business.

I have had one lawsuit at my commercial properties over the last eight years. Fundamentally, the tenant wanted me to replace 4 a/c systems even though three separate companies said they were operating correctly. We went to mediation and could not come to an agreement. After the mediation I decided to replace the 4 a/c units thinking this would end the lawsuit. This did **not** end the lawsuit. The tenant wanted me to pay $15,000 in legal fees that he had accumulated. My attorney said I would probably win the lawsuit in court, but I would probably end up paying my attorney $20,000 in legal fees to save $15,000. Even though I would most likely prevail in court, I paid the $15,000 in legal fees to be done with the lawsuit.

This is a good example of why there is a problem with lawsuits in this country. Individuals sue businesses for slip and fall or for other miscellaneous reasons. They know it is easier and cheaper for the business to just settle for $20,000 or $25,000 than to start paying the attorney to defend the lawsuit. This practice of paying off poor lawsuits is the main reason property and business insurance rates continue to increase rapidly.

What the State of Florida and many other states need is "Loser Pays". For instance, if you file a lawsuit and lose, you not only pay your attorney costs but you also pay the attorney costs of the defendant. This would end all the frivolous lawsuits. Obviously trial attorneys would be against this.

Part 2:
FOUR TRAITS TO YOUR SUCCESS

1. Perseverance and Dedication.
2. Communication Skills
3. Passion
4. Knowledge of industry

1. Perseverance and Dedication

Most important is perseverance and dedication, having the "do what it takes attitude" to become a success. When I started my Allstate insurance office, my motto was, *failure is not an option*. I actually took over an Allstate office that had failed.

That agent was intelligent and communicated effectively, but he was lazy. He did not have the perseverance and dedication to be successful. I had tried to help him and invited him to get involved with my dealership program. I wanted him to get involved in going to dealerships because, frankly, it can be a little intimidating going to dealerships on your own. Having two of us go into the dealership would have given me more confidence. He agreed, but every evening when we were supposed to meet, he backed out.

It was always the same excuse, "My wife wants me to go home for dinner."

I would tell him, "Dinner. Who cares about dinner? Eat later. We need to get to the dealerships to make some money."

He would always go home, and I would head to the dealerships. He failed, and I succeeded because of one thing. I had the perseverance and dedication to do what it takes to be a success.

Example: A friend was selling prescription drugs for Pfizer, earning approximately 90-100k per year. For most people that would be good; however, for my friend it was not good. He decided he wanted to work for a company that did a medical procedure during a heart by-pass operation. This company's procedure took veins from the leg to be used for the heart by-pass procedure.

My friend flew from Dallas to California to attend a national seminar with one goal in mind, to meet the owner of this particular company, give him a resume and setup an interview. Since there were thousands of people at this seminar, he printed out a picture of the owner and kept it in his pocket so the owner's image would be fresh in his mind. On the third and final day, my friend spotted the owner at the coffee station. He was able to have a small conversation with the owner and was able to setup an interview in a couple of weeks.

At the interview, my friend was told he had great communication skills. He had the knowledge and motivation to be a successful representative. There was just one point to be considered. My friend would need to be in the operating room, and there was a concern that all the blood from this invasive surgery might cause him to pass out during such a major procedure.

The owner raised the question, "How can I hire you if I do not even know how you would react to being in an operating room?"

My friend asked, "If I can be a witness to a heart by-pass operation in the next two weeks, will you give serious consideration to hiring me?"

The business owner agreed. My friend made it happen. A friend's mother was a nurse in the operating room in Atlanta, GA. He got approval from the surgeon and was off to Atlanta to view the surgery. Two weeks later he was hired, and his salary went up to $250,000 per year. This is a great example of perseverance and dedication.

Without this internal drive to succeed, whether it is in business, playing golf, or learning how to crochet, your perseverance and dedication to accomplish your goals is of utmost importance.

Many of the commercial property transactions and the title insurance business I am involved with took many months, and in some cases years, to bring together. These deals many times take a long time to put together because they have to be good for me. Obviously, I could put a deal together quickly; however, if it does not make financial success, why do the deal? If you believe in the new business, new property, or even new golf swing, you have to have the mental toughness to push forward no matter what happens.

Many times people get sidetracked by comments from family and friends and abandon their current project or goal. If negative comments bother you and affect your forward progress, stop telling these types of people your plans and goals. I can keep writing and writing, but perseverance comes down to your inner being and whether or not you will be resolute to make your goals happen.

2. Communication Skills

Communication skills are the second most important attribute. Communication is the ability to get things done. You cannot be afraid to talk with people, ask questions and resolve problems. If you are afraid to talk on the phone, how will you get things done, how will you find answers to problems? If you are afraid or tentative to speak on the phone, start calling someone every day or three times per week. You get better at any task by practicing it often; this is true whether you want to be a better bowler, hair stylist, or communicator.

When I was an Allstate agent I spoke to people all day long for years. It is no accident that speaking on the phone is one of my best skills. If speaking is an issue for you, and I think it's an issue for 90% of the population, I recommend joining Toastmasters. This organization is an inexpensive and time effective way to improve your speaking skills. I recommend it and am currently a member.

Good communicators can get other people to see their point of view and then get them to go along with it. Many times an issue or topic will have two points of view. As an excellent communicator you will be able to effectively explain why your view makes the most sense.

I am currently speaking with a tenant regarding a lease renewal and small increase in rent. The tenant is adamant that he is paying enough already. He is threatening to move and overall does not want to discuss the issue. As an effective communicator, while speaking to the tenant I am going to remain calm and speak clearly and concisely to explain why the rent payments I am requesting are still a good deal in the local market. I will also explain how our company is customer service oriented, and how we work hard to maintain our properties at a high level.

3. Passion

What are your goals in life, what do you enjoy doing? Many people I know really do not enjoy what they are doing. They would rather be doing something else the 40 or 50 hours a week they are at work. No matter what your passion is or what your interests are, you can start working toward your goals. No, it would not make sense to quit your job tomorrow to play video games or play basketball all day at the park. Nevertheless, you could start taking classes to be a video game programmer or start working up plans to start your own neighborhood youth basketball league.

My neighbor is really into soccer, so he started a recreational youth soccer league about 15 years ago. It has been a joy for him to operate since this is where his interest lies (his passion), and it has been a big positive for the community.

My passion once I was out of college was to make as much money as possible. It took many years to accomplish this goal, but I started working on it right out of college. The first thing I did was to enroll in a college to get a master's degree with a major in finance. I wanted to learn as much as possible about how the business and financial markets worked. The career paths I chose were based on the fact that I thought I could make a lot of money.

For example, I observed that a local wedding photographer made a lot of money. Soon after, I started a wedding videography business.

Another example is that one day my mom, who was a teller at a bank, told me that a State Farm insurance agent was always coming into the branch to deposit large checks. Before long I started working towards becoming an Allstate insurance agent. The goal of becoming an Allstate insurance agent was accomplished two years later.

Through talking with people and personal observance over the years I became convinced that owning commercial property was a path to financial freedom. After many years of research, personal initiative, and determination I purchased my first commercial office building in 2004.

Was becoming an Allstate agent, starting a wedding videography business, or purchasing a commercial property easy? No it was not, but I made it happen. The reason for success in changing your career path is mostly personal determination.

I have a friend who hates his job. Every time I see him I ask how the job is going. His response is always the same. He wishes he could do something else because this job is not for him. I then ask what he is doing to find a new line of work, and the answer is always, "nothing yet".

My guess is that my friend will never make a change to his career path. He will continue to hate his job for the next twenty years until he retires. *That is a fun way to live your life*! It is just too difficult for my friend to make a change to his normal daily routine. He does not have much personal determination. Remember, if you don't go after what you want, you will never have it.

Passion is useless if there is no action to pursue it. Most people can tell you their passion, but few people act on that passion. The goal is to match up your action (your job) with your passion.

I have talked to many people who are not enjoying their current job. I usually ask if they are looking for a change to a different job, and the answer is almost always no. I would like to ask each person why not?

It is amazing how many people continue along in a job position or career that they dislike or flat out hate. So the question is why do people do this? I believe there are two main reasons.

The first reason is that people are unmotivated or lazy. People have to be able to dig deep inside to find the motivation. No one can find it for them. Sometimes people are forced to get motivated when they lose their job. The current recession has helped many people to get motivated to find a job or start a business based on their passion in life.

My personal motivation was to make money and to live a more comfortable life than when I was growing up. Also, you live only once, so you might as well live it to the best of your abilities. On your deathbed you do not want to have any regrets.

The second reason is that people are afraid of change. It is natural for people to be afraid of the unknown. They start "what- if-ing" possible future problems. My wife started "what-if-ing" my first commercial property transaction.

She would say, "What if all the tenants leave? What if you need a new roof? What if a tenant falls in the parking lot and sues us?"

My response was, "What if the world comes to an end tomorrow, and then we will not have to worry about any of this."

But, seriously, I told her if this was going to cause her too much stress I would not go forward with the property purchase.

My wife finally said, "Go ahead with the purchase, and I will not what if you anymore." She has upheld her promise, and now eight years later she has not "what-if-d" me on any other transaction.

The fact is that on these property transactions I do my homework (due diligence), so I am making decisions based on extensive research. When the research steers me to purchase a property or business, I go forward with the transaction and do not change my mind because I get scared, worried or for any other emotional reason.

4. Knowledge of Industry

It is important to become as knowledgeable as possible in the business you are about to start. Take advantage of other people's expertise, including the pitfalls they have encountered. Subscribe to magazines in your field, do online research, talk to other people currently in the business.

If the part about becoming knowledgeable in your field is a hassle or you find you are not interested, maybe this field or type of business is not your passion. Your expertise in your industry will expand rapidly once you have started your business. Yes, become as knowledgeable as possible, but do not let the fact that you are not an expert stop you from starting your business. People who want to be business owners sometimes think that others who already own businesses have some kind of hidden talent or gift. The fact is most people are about the same, and it comes down to perseverance and dedication, communication skills, passion, and knowledge of industry. These four characteristics will determine your success.

Part 3:
My Business Ventures

My first business startup:

AB Creative Videography

Most of my business ventures usually occur by observing other successful businesses. One does not have to reinvent the wheel to be successful, and in many cases you can actually copy a business. My dad's friend did wedding photography as a side business. It was well known that he made quite a bit of money on this side business, probably four or five times more than from his day job. This reinforced the idea that owning your own business is the way to go. I thought this was an opportunity to start a weekend business and make some decent money.

After further research (due diligence), we decided to start a wedding videography business instead of a wedding photography business. Having little knowledge of the wedding business, it seemed to me there would be a lot more competition doing wedding photography as well as more stress over goofing up a couple's wedding pictures.

The stepson of my dad's friend worked for a wedding videography business and agreed to let us follow him around for two weddings. The information we gathered was priceless. In one evening of following around a professional wedding videographer I had learned enough to get our business started.

This philosophy can be applied in other fields. If you want to open a coffee shop, go work at Starbucks for a month. Work at a hair salon for a month if you want to open a hair salon. Learn as much as you can about how the business operates. You do not need to tell your employer that your motive is to open a coffee shop or hair salon down the street.

Did I know everything about wedding videography at this time? Of course not, but I would learn along the way. Many people never start a business because they keep researching and researching about the industry and waiting for a planet to align with Jupiter. Often, too much research causes confusion and second guessing. I am not a big fan of creating a business plan. A business plan contains too many made up variables and takes too much time to complete. Am I saying to blindly start a business? Of course not.

After all the comments of family and friends that we could not and should not start the business, I pushed forward and started the business. I used all the money we had received from our own wedding one year earlier, about $4,000, to purchase video equipment. This left me with video equipment, no money in the bank and no customers. Now what? At the time, the internet was too new and of no help.

We became familiar with the wedding industry in the Detroit, MI area. We put a table up at a Target event that was free. This is where we found our first customer without spending any money on advertising. We agreed to videotape the wedding for $500, which was a low price even back in 1995. We had to start somewhere, and this first job started things rolling. I thought if we could get a few jobs and get our names out there things would take off.

The business did take off, mostly through word of mouth, and we were doing 35 weddings a year at about $1200 per wedding in our third year in business. Pretty good for a part-time weekend business. It was not luck that made the business successful; it was providing good service and a good product at a good price. As simple as that! This successful business came about by doing my homework on the business (due diligence) and then going ahead and starting the business even though I was told by many not to do it.

TAKE AWAY: Do your homework, and don't let others tell you that you cannot do it.

TRAITS: Perseverance and Determination
Knowledge of Industry

What? You Want To Be a College professor?

Many times accomplishing things in life is not because you're the best or necessarily deserve something. It often comes down to perseverance. In 1995 I wanted to become a college professor. My first thought was, how will I accomplish this task? I applied for a few positions that I saw in the industry magazine, *The Chronicles of Higher Education*. These applications went nowhere; there were probably 500 people applying for each of the openings.

Yes, I had a Master's Degree in Finance but no doctorate degree and no teaching experience. Prospects were not looking good. How could I get in the front door? Every Sunday I looked through the employment classified ads for job openings to keep in touch with what was happening in the job market even though I was not looking for a job. One Sunday I noticed a small three line notice advertising a teaching position at a local college. I called the number, and the Dean of Business agreed that I could come in for an interview. At the interview I was told the school was looking for an English and computer instructor. My Master's Degree in Finance would not work. I thanked the dean for the interview and walked out the door.

Was I done pursuing a teaching position at this college? NO WAY! Every month, without fail, I went back to speak with the dean. I wanted to show my commitment to teaching at the college. Did I call ahead of time? No. The dean would have had nothing new to say, if I could have spoken with him at all. When I walked in the front door someone had to speak with me, and usually it was the dean.

Month after month I made the 30-minute trek to the college to attempt to talk with the dean. I continued to be turned down. By the fourth visit we were becoming friends, that is the dean and me. He started smiling when he saw me. I know he was thinking, are you here again, you never give up.

On the eighth visit I was finally hired. Was I the most qualified? Of course not. Nonetheless, the most persistent person, me, was offered the job. I, Kevin Erwin, was now a college professor. On the visit when I was offered the position, I walked into the dean's office and was asked to take a seat. That was a good sign which had not happened before. The dean and I made some small talk for a few minutes before he opened his desk and pulled out a thick folder and started looking through it. There was silence at this point. Was he pulling out a restraining order so I would stop bothering him?

Finally he looked up at me and asked, "Would you teach English?"

I said, "That is about the only class I would decline."

"How about teaching computers?" he asked.

"I will do it!" I thanked him for the opportunity.

As I was walking out the dean said, "By the way, what kind of degree do you have?"

"Finance," I responded.

I was so persistent that I was hired, having only a finance degree, to teach a computer class. I had very little computer background to qualify me to teach computers but thought I could figure it out, and I did.

Funny story-

About one year into teaching at this college, the dean asked if I could help teach an extra computer class, Word Perfect to be exact. I agreed. On the first day of class I began to teach Word Perfect.

Twenty minutes into the class a student raised his hand and proclaimed, "This class is not Word Perfect. It is Microsoft Word."

The dean had accidently given me the incorrect information. So there I was, suddenly standing in front of 40 students and having no knowledge of Microsoft Word. In fact, I had never even used it. Many of the students probably knew more about Microsoft Word than I, but I was supposed to teach the class.

It was at this point I told the class, "We are going to take a 20 minute break."

I then rushed to the bookstore to get the teacher's manual, sat down, and tried to figure out what I was doing. I made it through the first class, and by the end of the semester I was an expert in Microsoft Word.

TAKE AWAY: Don't give up so easily.
TRAITS: Perseverance and Determination
Communication Skills

Farthing: Residential Rental

Investing in commercial real estate is much more profitable than residential real estate. Commercial properties are also much easier to manage. The commercial tenant will be a business owner who wants to take care of the property because that is where he earns his money. Many times the residential tenant has the attitude that this is not my house and I am only going to live here one or two years so who cares what happens to this house. It is much easier to evict commercial tenants as opposed to residential tenants, as my story below will show.

Let's also consider the property maintenance issue with residential and commercial properties. In a home you are renting out, you have one tenant paying monthly rent. With this one tenant in this one home, you have to be concerned about the one roof. In a commercial property you could have ten tenants under one roof. When involved in residential investing, to have ten tenants you would need ten houses with ten roofs. That is a lot of roofs to maintain, repair, or replace.

I have a friend who has about 40 residential homes which he leases out. He had to hire two full-time employees to keep up with making repairs, getting new tenants, or evicting tenants who stopped paying their rent. With 40 commercial rentals, you could easily manage it on your own.

If you still want to have residential rental properties, here is one strategy for a young investor that I used twenty years ago. First, you purchase a home to live in. After moving in you start looking for another home to purchase. When you find a second home to purchase, tell the bank you will be moving into this second house so you can get a regular home loan. You **do** move into this second home. You will rent out your first home, but you don't need to tell the bank that.

If you were trying to get a loan for an investment property, it would be much more difficult than getting a regular home loan. The interest rate would be higher on an investment loan, and you would have to put a lot more money down.

After purchasing the second home, go out and purchase a third home and follow the same process. So, after the third home purchase, you have two rental properties and live in the third home. You will have three home loans as if you lived in each home. The bank could force you to get an investment loan if they ever found out you were not living in the house; however, that will not happen because you pay your bills on time each month. This is a quick way to get residential investment properties.

With a residential investment property you want to look for a house under $150,000 in a stable area with good public schools. The home that you purchase should be a standard type of house that fits in with the neighborhood. Do not purchase the odd-ball house. We looked for ranch houses that had three bedrooms and 1½ or 2 full bathrooms. This is the type of house that a young couple with one child would like to rent.

We had a residential rental house in Michigan, and the tenants stopped paying their rent. They had an option to purchase the home for $125,000. We made the mistake of listening to their excuses for four months before we took action to start the eviction process. We filed the wrong paperwork at first, and it took two more months to figure that out. We now had not received a rent payment in six months. Since we were inexperienced with evictions, we hired an attorney to get the deadbeat tenants evicted. Three months later we received the court ruling that the tenant must vacate the premises. By this time we hadn't received rent in ten months.

Someone from the Sheriff's Office went to the house to give the tenants notice that they had two days to vacate. The Sheriff agreed to meet me at the house two days later to make sure that they had vacated the house so I would not be walking into the house alone to face an angry tenant. When the Sheriff and I walked in we saw that they had, in fact, left but had destroyed the house. There was damage to the walls, missing fixtures, broken glass and clothing strewn throughout the house. They had also ripped up and taken all of the landscaping from the front yard. In two weeks, at a cost of $10,000, we were able to bring the house back to good condition. We had the last laugh, though. We ended up putting the property on the market and sold it for $148,000. That is $23,000 more than we were going to sell it to the renters who had the option to purchase.

TAKE AWAY: Commercial rentals are easier to manage and more profitable than residential. Evict non-paying tenants promptly.

TRAITS: This is one venture where I learned all of these traits.

Allstate Agent

In 1995 I became an Allstate agent, but it was not easy. I interviewed three times with Allstate. The first two attempts failed because the Allstate representative who was supposed to meet with me did not even show up. After the third interview, Allstate decided to hire me, but first I had to take an internal Allstate test. The test was supposed to measure the likelihood I would be successful as an Allstate insurance agent. I took the test twice and failed both times.

Allstate then told me that I could not be hired as an Allstate insurance agent but could try again in one year. I could not understand how a company test was going to dictate my ability to be a successful agent. As this meeting ended, I stood up from the chair, said goodbye, and headed to the door of the office. I opened the door, walked out and was about to shut the door behind me when my brain said, do not give up yet.

Instead of leaving, I poked my head back inside the office and said, "I know I will be successful and you know I will be successful so there has to be something you can do to help me become an agent. I just cannot believe we are letting a computer program decide my future with this company."

She looked me in the eyes, there was silence, and I could see her brain was thinking. I then heard, "Take a seat. I may have another option for you."

I ended up working for an existing Allstate agent for six months. This would be a real world test, not a computer program, to determine if I could sell property and casualty insurance. I was now determined to prove the computer program wrong. Selling this type of insurance as a new agent is not an easy task. Most new agents fail. The company's idea of marketing is called tele-marketing, calling people out of the clear blue and trying to sell auto insurance. This method to me is a ridiculous waste of time and is very ineffective.

The most effective method I discovered was the auto dealership program. Why not go to a place where people needed auto insurance to drive off the lot and were actually interested in discussing insurance?

I had heard of a very successful agent about 10 miles away. In fact, he was the most successful agent in the region. My first question was how does this agent sell so much insurance? I was told he sold auto insurance at dealerships, but my territory supervisor told me this was not good insurance business and would be a bad idea for me to pursue. My underwriter told me there were a lot of claims with dealership business.

I was being advised against copying what the highest paid agent was doing. This made no sense to me. I was going through all the hard work of selling insurance to make a lot of money. Why else would I sell insurance? It is not fun or particularly rewarding. So I followed someone else's successes and set up my own auto dealership insurance program.

I followed someone else's successful sales strategy. I did not have to think up an entire new sales strategy or re-invent the wheel. I basically copied another person's successful strategy and tried to make it better.

The dealership program became very successful; I became one of the most successful new agents for the company. Basically the way it worked was when a salesperson at a dealership needed auto insurance for a new or used car sale, he called me. I would jump in my car, drive to the dealership, and sell a new auto insurance policy on the spot. The salesperson sold the car right away before the customer started having second thoughts, and I sold a new insurance policy.

I also brought the dealerships pizza for lunch once per week. The important thing about the pizza is that I did not just drop it off and leave; I sat down and ate lunch with the sales staff each and every week. I not only became the guy who sold insurance, I also became friends with everyone in the dealership. The key is that I developed personal relationships with the sales staff. Within a couple of years it got to the point where I was eating pizza for lunch two or three times per day.

I also brought the female salespeople large chocolate bars. You would have thought I was bringing them bars of gold instead of bars of chocolate with all the excitement created when I walked in with the chocolate.

Because personal relationships were built with the auto dealerships and the food deliveries were constant, I had no worries that a competitor would swoop in and steal my business. I was able to prove that the Allstate computer program was not so smart in deciding who would be a successful insurance agent. Personal initiative and determination were the key attributes to success. I was determined from day one. Failure as an Allstate agent was not an option. This is the attitude that a new business owner must have.

TAKE AWAY: Look at what other successful people are doing in that industry.

TRAITS: Perseverance and Determination
Communication Skills
Passion

Golf Course

In 2000, it became obvious that my career at Allstate was coming to an end. The company began raising premiums on the insurance policies anywhere from 25 to 75 percent and began putting heavy pressure on the agents to sell disability insurance. I did not mind the increase if the company would have allowed us to sell insurance through another company at the same time. Many customers were leaving my agency because of the exorbitant price increases. At this same time the territory manager was telling me I had to sell a large amount of disability insurance, or I would be fired. It was then that I realized I needed to apply my perseverance and determination to another venture. I began to come up with my next plan.

I initially wanted to purchase a golf course and get out of the insurance business. I found several brokers who only dealt with golf courses and started researching every golf course that was for sale east of the Mississippi River. After about two months I was beginning to figure out the type of golf course that I thought would be profitable and fit within my budget. If the opportunity arose, I would contact the owners of the golf course and ask them every question I could think of. I was quickly gaining knowledge of the industry; doing my due diligence.

At this point I started visiting golf courses in person to ask more questions and to possibly consider an offer if I liked what I saw. Sometimes I would show up early, like a day early, to look at the golf course so the owner could not cover up anything before my scheduled arrival.

One particular incident comes to mind. A golf course went up for sale on the east side of Charlotte, North Carolina on a Thursday morning. Since I had been studying golf courses that were for sale over the last several months, I knew that this type of course was what I was looking for. So I had to look at the course, pronto. If it was a good deal, it would be sold quickly.

At about 1:00 pm on Friday, I jumped into my Honda Accord with my 16 year old brother-in-law to make the trip to see the golf course. By Friday night we made it to somewhere in Kentucky from Detroit, MI. We decided to get a hotel room and continue our journey in the morning. The next day we left at 8:00 am and finally arrived at the golf course at 4:30 pm. When we arrived at the course, it was lightly raining, was beginning to get dark since it was the first week of December, and was about 40 degrees outside. The only car in the parking lot belonged to the manager of the club. He had been told by the owner to wait for us.

As I pulled into the parking lot, I rolled down the window and said, "Get us a cart, we are playing golf."

He thought I was kidding, since it was cold, raining, and would be dark in about 1½ hours.

I said, "We just drove 800 miles, and we are playing golf and checking out this golf course!"

We played all 18 holes in the next 1½ hours in the rain and cold. The manager was still waiting for us when we finished. By this time he was not very happy, but I still asked him to show me around the clubhouse and every other building that was owned by the business.

By 8:00 pm I had done all of the due diligence I could handle for the day. My brother-in-law and I headed into downtown Charlotte to find a hotel for the night. On the way to the hotel, I received a call from my wife saying a huge snowstorm was on the way that evening, and we would most likely be stranded in Charlotte, North Carolina for two or three days. Instead of being stranded in Charlotte, we drove through the night back to Cleveland, OH and arrived at my brother's house at 5:30 am Sunday morning.

Why do I tell this story? To show what I would go through to purchase a golf course. This is the kind of dedication you will need to start a new business and be successful. Perseverance and dedication are required.

Did I purchase the golf course? No. The back nine of the course is a very poor setup. I would not have known this had I not played all eighteen holes in the cold, rainy weather. Also, the course was located too far out in the country. This course would be successful in a highly populated area. To convince golfers to drive 30 minutes, the golf course has to be worth the trip, and this course would not be worth the trip.

TAKE AWAY: Do your homework and be willing to jump through hoops to get the answers you need.

TRAITS: Perseverance and Determination
Passion
Knowledge of Industry

Evans Insurance

In 2002 I sold the Allstate Insurance business and purchased an independent insurance agency in Kissimmee, FL. Looking back, I realize I did not do enough due diligence on this business. I was more concerned about moving to sunny Florida. The business was in more disarray than I thought; nonetheless, I was able to turn it around in six months. It took a lot, and I mean a lot, of work.

One year into this new venture I realized that the property and casualty business was no longer my passion. In 2003 a local Allstate agent walked in my office and stated he wanted to purchase the business. After convincing me he was serious, I told him the price I would accept for my business. He said the price was good with him and that he would work on getting financing. Two weeks later he called to tell me that he could not find financing and that he did not have enough funds to pay cash.

I thought that this was the end of the deal. Six months later, however, on December 1, 2003, he called me on the phone to tell me he had found financing. The deal had to be closed by the end of the year so on the last business day of 2003 the paperwork was signed, at my full asking price of course.

TAKE AWAY: Are you doing what you love? Are you passionate about it?
TRAITS: Passion

Colonial Park

The first commercial property I purchased after my insurance days was called Colonial Park. I decided commercial property was a good business for me since I would not have to be actively involved on a daily basis. In other words, I did not have to clock in at 9:00 am every day. Yes, the commercial property keeps me busy; however, I work at my own pace, and I can do the majority of the work when I decide to fit it into my schedule. Also, my observation over the years has been that property owners tend to be wealthy. See picture below:

This is a 6900 square foot office building that sits on a main road in a growing area. The only particularly interesting thing that happened with this property is that two months after I purchased it Hurricane

Charley ripped half the roof off and damaged all the signage, among other things. I remember driving to the property with my wife a day after the storm. On the way I started thinking my wife might be upset if she saw our building all torn apart. I explained to her that no matter what the property looked like she should remember we had insurance. She still became a little emotional when she saw the property; I guess it is human nature.

Do not go one day without your property or business being insured. You never know what will happen. Commercial property insurance and business insurance are relatively inexpensive. There should be enough coverage to rebuild the property as well as, in my opinion, at least one million in liability coverage.

Make sure the company you purchase the insurance from has a high stability rating from Moody's or S&P. Moody's and S&P rate companies on their strength or likelihood they will go out of business. It will do no good to have insurance if the company goes out of business due to a bad storm or hurricane. Get at least three quotes to find your best deal.

Another incident that proved to be a learning experience was when a pipe broke in the wall at one of the offices. The office was flooded within minutes. All the flooring was ruined. Again, this building was insured and we fixed the flooring in one week with as little disruption to the business as possible.

The second day after the leak I started hearing the word "mold" among the business owners. Don't get me wrong, mold can be a problem. In most cases, however, it is blown way out of proportion. This is another reason I wanted to dry up the floor and get the new flooring in as soon as possible.

At this time a business owner three doors down called to tell me there was mold in the bathroom. The leak was nowhere near this unit, but the owner had the word mold in her mind so all of a sudden she had a mold issue. She had leased the space for two years. Upon viewing the bathroom, I saw two quarter size black spots. I knew from experience there was not a mold problem, but the tenant was not going to just believe me.

I cut out all of the sheet rock (drywall) from the floor to two feet up. I asked the tenant to look inside the walls for any sign of mold. There was no mold. The walls were repaired. Even though this cost me money and I knew it was a waste of time, I knew the tenant was not going to get mold off her mind until I proved to her there was no mold. The business owner went back to being a happy tenant telling everyone I was great. If I had not done anything about the mold, even though it was a waste of time, the tenant would have continued telling everyone she had mold problems that I was not correcting. The "so called" mold issue could have spread to other businesses. There would have been a negative vibe or attitude spreading through the office building. Sometimes you have to do things that make people happy for the long term good.

TAKE AWAY: Don't be afraid of change. Don't "What If?" yourself out of success. Always insure your property. Keep your tenants happy.

TRAITS: Communication Skills
Knowledge of Industry

Lady Lake

This property in Lady Lake, FL was one of the first properties I looked at many years ago. At the time I was still the owner of Evans Insurance and had just started to learn about commercial properties. Now I was learning as much as I could about commercial properties.

I had a property developer friend go out to this property with me to give me some advice. The seller was asking $500,000 for this 7,000 square foot strip center. The property was run down but structurally sound, and it was in an above average area. All of the a/c systems looked old and in very poor condition. After reviewing everything about the property, I did not purchase it because of the a/c systems. Looking back, I believe that was a dumb reason not to purchase the property.

One month after dismissing this property as unacceptable due to the a/c systems, I called the realtor back to say I would like to purchase the property for $500,000. The realtor told me the owner no longer wanted to sell. I started calling the realtor back every month to ask if the owner had changed his mind. About one year later the owner finally changed his mind, but he now wanted $600,000. The new price was still a good deal, so the contract was signed two days later before the owner changed his mind again.

Shortly after signing the contract, the owner did have second thoughts. He increased the asking price by $100,000 on the MLS listing, Loopnet, and the Property Source Book. Loopnet is the most popular online website to learn of commercial properties for sale. The owner was also not returning phone calls to me or the broker. He was now thinking he had underpriced the property, and he was right.

While I was inspecting the property with an inspection company, a realtor was showing the property to another buyer. I asked the realtor what was going on and told her the property was already under contract. She was surprised and did not seem to believe me. The owner had hired a new real estate broker to sell this property. I informed the realtor again that this property was sold with the closing planned in about 20 days.

After meeting the new realtor, I called the original realtor who had helped me sign the contract to tell him the owner was obviously not cooperating, was ignoring us, and was actively trying to sell the property for a higher price. The owner wanted us to go away. Unfortunately for him, we had a signed contract. What should I do next? The owner was not cooperating, and it is always difficult to purchase a property without both the buyer and the seller concurring.

Yes, I could contact an attorney and start paying $150-$200 per hour for legal assistance. The realtor knew the property owner's attorney, and we were guessing that he was going to use him for this transaction. I called the attorney and explained to him that we had a fully signed contract and were going to purchase the property but had not been able to contact the owner over the last week. I also explained that the owner was still actively marketing and showing the property, and we were afraid he was trying to back out of our deal. After this talk with the owner's attorney, the owner started communicating with us again. Apparently the attorney contacted the owner and explained to him that there was a legally binding contract for the sale of the property and that he could not just pretend a contract was not signed. Fifteen days later we purchased the property.

We updated the property with several new a/c systems and also put stucco on the front of the building along with a fresh coat of paint and new electric signs above each unit. The stucco, paint, and signs vastly improved the look of the building, and it was relatively inexpensive. The tenants were so happy they did not seem to mind a small increase in rent. The local city has a beautification committee that nominated me for *Improved Property of the Year*. I felt like I was the local hero for bringing this property back to life.

The property remained fully leased for the first two years with only one constant complaint coming from the tenants. The complaint was that the dirt and gravel parking lot in back of the building was unacceptable. I decided to do something about it. I received three quotes to pave this small ten space parking lot and picked a $10,000 quote from a company I felt would do a good job. The asphalt parking lot was completed. The lot looked good, and the tenants loved it.

Unfortunately, two weeks later I was notified that the city did not care for the new parking lot. The problem was I did not pull the proper permit. The city not only wanted a permit but also approval from the local water management council verifying that the retention pond was large enough so there would not be any flooding at the property. I asked if someone from the city could meet me at the property so they could see with their own eyes that the retention pond was four times as big as the parking lot and the property would not flood in a million years. The city refused to meet me and reiterated that I needed approval of the local water management district.

I contacted an engineer who dealt with these water issues to find out how to get this resolved. The engineer told me that since the water council was a government entity the approval process could easily take six months or more and cost me $20,000 in engineering and legal fees. I was also informed that if I applied for approval to the water management council they would evaluate the entire property not just the back area with the small parking lot. Their evaluation would be to see if the property met the government's flooding standards. What I learned was that after the evaluation took place, it was possible I would have to tear up all of the front parking lot if I did not meet government flooding standards.

The ruling by the water management council had the potential of literally destroying the property and forcing the tenants to move out. The power of government. Amazing! I saw this issue as conceivably turning into a large problem for me. I contacted the asphalt company that installed the parking lot and had them remove it the following week. The issue with the city was resolved, and the tenants were back to the dirt and gravel parking lot.

I was so fed up after this issue that I decided to sell. Looking back, I realize this was probably an overreaction. I found a buyer at a price of $875,000, and this property was sold. The lesson I took from this experience was that when you are looking at a property to purchase and the parking lot is gravel, keep in mind that it may not be easy or possible to install a parking lot due to government regulations and the permits that are required.

TAKE AWAY: Don't let old air conditioning units stop you from buying a property. Know what the government regulations are concerning gravel parking lots.

TRAITS: Perseverance and Determination
Communication Skills
Passion
Knowledge of Industry

Winter Haven

This commercial property came up for sale one morning as I was looking through my list of new properties on the market. I knew this property was a good deal, a 12,000 square foot retail center, fully leased, and very close to the Cypress Gardens Amusement Park. Within an hour I was in my car to make the 90 minute trip to the property. This property was selling for $83 per square foot for a total of $1 million, a good price in 2005. The property needed a little updating, but most importantly it was structurally sound and located in an above average location. This was a bargain. From the parking lot I dialed the real estate agent to tell him I would like to make an offer.

The broker informed me, "It's already sold."

"How can it be sold already? It was just listed five hours ago." I said.

The broker and I ended up talking for about an hour on the phone while I was sitting in the car at the property. I ended the conversation by telling the broker I would like to do a full price back up offer. He said he would fax over the backup contract. One week went by. I did not receive the backup offer contract, so I called the agent back and asked if he was still going to send it to me.

He then told me about the games the buyer was playing. The buyer did not want to pay the state fees, amounting to about $9,000, associated with the transaction. Normally the seller pays this state fee, but everything is negotiable. The buyer had faxed the contract back to the broker without signing it. It was at this point that I had happened to call the broker back.

The broker asked me, "Do you want the deal? I am tired of playing games with the other buyer."

My response was, "Of course."

By the end of the day I had a contract on the property. It was a full price offer of $1,000,000, and I was going to be paying the $9,000 dollar state fee. It was such a good deal I was not concerned with the $9,000 dollar state fee, and I had not even looked at the leases. The contract gave me 20 days due diligence to look over the property, so I could get out of it for any reason during the first 20 days. For right now the important thing was the contract was signed.

timing is everything:
Yes, I had good timing in making the follow up call to the broker that ultimately landed me the deal. But this deal would not have happened if my phone communication skills were not good. In my first phone call I was able to develop a good rapport and trust with the broker that I was a good person with whom to do a property transaction. Yes, good timing can be lucky, but you must put yourself in a position to take advantage of the luck. I define luck as **opportunity met with preparation.** During that second phone call, when the broker asked me if I wanted the deal, I had enough knowledge of the commercial property industry to say yes instantly. All those hours of researching properties and miles driving to different properties had just paid off.

Interesting story-
Around the same time as the last property purchase, I entered into a contract to purchase a small office plaza in Punta Gorda, FL. On paper this property fit the criteria I had in mind. In this particular case I sent a purchase contract over first without looking at the property since it was a six hour drive (round trip) to view the property. If the owner rejected my offer, I would just move on to the next property and not waste a day driving to look at this one. The owner accepted my offer in this instance, and we entered into a binding contract. Of course I had 20 days due diligence to get out of the deal. The seller, on the other hand, could not legally get out of the deal. I decided to go look at the property the next Monday.

During the weekend, however, I found another property that would work better for me and decided to get out of the Punta Gorda deal with the due diligence clause. For whatever reason, I decided to wait until Wednesday of the next week to call the broker to tell him the property was not suitable for me. As luck would have it, I received a call from the owner on Tuesday saying he had made a mistake and did not want to sell the property after all. You guessed right! I now wanted to purchase the property, and we still had a legal contract allowing me to do so. If they had just waited one more day, I would have cancelled the contract and it would have been terminated. The seller ended up paying us $15,000 to get out of the deal. Not bad for doing nothing. Timing was good in this situation.

TAKE AWAY: There is nothing lucky about luck. **Luck is opportunity met with preparation.**

TRAITS: Perseverance and Determination
Communication Skills
Passion
Knowledge of Industry

Small storage facility

I located a small storage facility in the Tampa Bay, FL area. The cash flow seemed good, and it was in a growing area. The purchase price was $500,000 with a deposit of $12,000. On the last day of due diligence, the day I could cancel the contract and get my deposit money back, a lender verbally assured me they could do the deal. I was told they could not send a written confirmation because the vice president of commercial lending had to sign off on the deal, and he was out of town. They reassured me over and over again that this deal was no problem; they could definitely do it. So I did not cancel the contract, and my due diligence was over.

Three days later the loan officer called. "I made a mistake," he stated, "I cannot do the deal."

I soon found out that finding a loan for this small storage facility would be difficult. One loan officer told me his concern was that a large company would come into the area and build a huge facility. They would then set the prices so low it could drive the small operators of storage facilities out of business. This made sense to me since the location of a storage facility is not as important as the location of a retail strip center. Based on this, I decided to lose my security deposit and move on to another deal.

What I learned was that sometimes you will lose money by taking a risk; this is going to happen. I also learned to commit to lower deposits unless I am trying to prove to an owner I am serious about purchasing a property. Sometimes presenting an offer with a large deposit check attached to it can make a difference.

Bunker Hill

When purchased, it looked like this:

After updating:

Sometimes the best way to purchase a property is to just contact the property owner directly. I contacted the owner of the Bunker Hill strip center and asked if he wanted to sell. The owner was older and said he would sell for $2 million, which was way above the $1.4 million I thought it was worth. This started a conversation that went back and forth for six months. After a year we still could not agree on price, but it was becoming evident that the older gentleman was going to need help in managing the property.

The owner's son asked if I could help with the bookkeeping. I agreed to start managing the property for him, not for the little amount of money I received each month but so eventually I could purchase the property. Six months into managing the property, I was accused by a local real estate agent of illegally managing a commercial property because I did not have a real estate license. More government intrusion! The owner of the property and I contacted an attorney to look into this claim. The attorney came back with an inconclusive answer. I decided to tell the property owner I could not manage his property because I was not sure if I was doing something illegal and did not want to risk that I was.

It only took a few days for the property owner to call me back and let me know he was ready to sell for the price I had offered. The contract was signed, and we closed four weeks later. I updated the property with new paint, stucco work, new signage, and a new 500 gallon water tank for the well.

The tenants took a few weeks to adapt to the way I managed the property. I required a new lease if the current one was terminated and made it clear that the lease payments were due on the first day of the month and would be considered late if the payment was not received by the 10th day of the month. The tenants eventually became used to paying during the first week of the month and not when they felt like it. You want your tenant to feel that his lease payment is the most important bill to pay and that it should be paid before the water, electric, and any other bill.

The property next to ours was a convenience store. Due to the way the properties sit, many people used our parking lot as a cut through to get to the convenience store. This caused two problems for our property. The constant flow of cars was a liability issue for people walking in the parking lot, and there were constantly teenagers wandering onto our property while hanging out around the convenience store.

One wood fence ended this problem. On the day the fence was being installed, one of the business owners (tenants) came out. In a loud voice he told me that I was out of my mind to put a fence up that blocked traffic and that it would become too difficult for customers to get to our property. He said that he may have to move or go out of business.

Calmly I explained, "It's just a fence. Let's give it a try, and if it causes problems we will take it down in a couple of weeks."

Less than one week later the same business owner called to tell me that the fence was a great idea after all. There was no longer a constant flow of cars, and no teenagers were hanging out on the property. It probably helped business because customers did not have to be concerned about tattooed teenagers or what problems might be encountered.

TAKE AWAY: Sometimes you have to invest time and effort into something before you see the payoff.

TRAITS: Perseverance and Determination

Communication Skills

Passion

Knowledge of Industry

T-shirt Business

I decided to start a t-shirt business with my daughter to show her how a business works. The first thing we had to do was come up with a business name. We picked Jinxtee. At the time, the word Jinx was popular at her elementary school. We then checked the Florida website, sunbiz.org, to see if the name was already taken. After finding out it was available, we signed up online. We then went to the Federal Government website (Irs.gov) to get our Fed ID number. Ten minutes later we had our Fed ID number and we were open for business, kind of.

We decided to turn the t-shirt business into a monthly contest. The contest involved people submitting t-shirt designs to us, and once per month we would pick a winning design. The winner would receive $25 and a t-shirt with the winning design. Once we had the first winning design, we had to find the best company to make the t-shirts. We found a company to make 100 t-shirts at $5 each. We are selling the t-shirts for $10 each.

We have not sold many t-shirts, and the business is currently on hold. The business has essentially stopped operating because of a lack of passion. I was hoping my daughter would become interested in the t-shirt business. It has not happened, and my wife and I have lost interest also. This goes back to having the passion to make your business successful. If I had the passion for the t-shirt business, there is no doubt in my mind it would be successful. Remember, failure in my mind is not an option.

Title Insurance Business

During one of my property purchases I was referred to a local title insurance agency to do the closing. They did such a good job I started using them on every property transaction that I could; of course, the seller normally decides which title company will close the transaction. But, remember, everything is negotiable. As the years went by I began to get to know the closers of this particular title insurance office. It became obvious to me that they were well known in the community, did many transactions each month, and made a lot of money for the large company for which they worked.

I approached the managers (closers) that I knew and asked if they would like to start a new title insurance business. My offer was that I would invest monetarily to help get the business up and running. They would be leaving a large national company to start a small title office from scratch. I kept asking on and off over a two year time frame.

In August 2009 I purchased an office condo and thought that this would be a good place to open a title insurance office. I had not talked with the two managers for about six months, but this would be a good time to make one more call. This call would prove to be good timing. Employees of the local office where the managers worked were being forced to work through a national call center. To call someone at that local office first you had to speak with someone at the national call center and then they would, hopefully, forward you to the right person at the right office in a timely manner. Is this bad customer service or what? You would think a large national company would not goof up like this.

With the company going to the call center, the two managers took my offer, and we began making plans to start a new title insurance agency. Our plan was to be open for business in December 2009. In the middle of November the large title company found out about our plans through the grapevine and fired the entire staff instantly. We had not done anything illegal, and the employees were all going to give their two week notice.

Approximately three weeks before we were going to open, all of the employees were standing there at the new office, looking at me as I walked in. At this point we had no computers, telephone system or copiers. One bright spot, we did have furniture. Within ten days we were up and running. It has now been two and a half years since we opened the title insurance business. Things are going well; of course, it could always be better.

There are a lot of opportunities out there. Sometimes just by keeping your eyes and ears open you will find a good opportunity.

Here is a picture of our office:

TAKE AWAY: Establish connections in the field and community. You never know when a connection or relationship you built years ago will come into play in your future.

TRAITS: Perseverance and Determination
Communication Skills
Passion
Knowledge of Industry

Mt. Dora Property

In 2007, I spotted a 4,000 square foot strip center for sale in Mt. Dora, FL.

I called the owner who was also the listing agent; the property was listed for $700,000. After looking over the property, including the financials, I offered $500,000. The offer was declined without a counter offer. Six months went by. I called the owner back and found out he would sell for $650,000 now. I told them that price would still not work for me. I called back six months later. He would now sell for $600,000, still not good enough. Another year went by, and I followed up with a phone call. I learned he would now sell for $500,000. Good news! Right? No, not good news.

By this time the real estate market had collapsed. I did another analysis of the property and determined the current value was $350,000; of course, the owner rejected my offer. He should have accepted my offer of $500,000 two years earlier.

Another year went by so it was now the summer of 2010, and I decided to give the owner another phone call. The phone number I had been using was now disconnected so I decided to take a drive to the property and check it out. While talking with a few of the tenants I learned that the owner had retired and moved to Kentucky. I was also told that the bank was foreclosing on the property.

The tenants were unhappy because the general maintenance at the property was becoming neglected. They were especially discontented that the septic system was in poor condition and needed to be replaced. This current news was good for me, the potential buyer. One of the tenants gave me the owner's new phone number in Kentucky. I called the owner and was told he would now sell the property for $425,000. He was in agreement that the septic had to be replaced at a cost of $25,000. I offered $325,000, with the owner replacing the septic system.

The negotiations went back and forth over the next two months without an agreement. I was in the driver's seat since I knew the owner was getting close to foreclosure. The owner's final offer was $275,000, but he wanted me to hand him an additional $50,000 in cash in the parking lot after closing. I think this is illegal, definitely unethical. He wanted the cash outside of closing because whatever amount was collected at closing was going to the bank to pay down the lien, and he would receive nothing.

The first question one would ask is, "how was the owner going bankrupt if this strip center is fully leased?" He had taken out one large loan with several properties involved. Even though this particular property was doing well, the owner's properties as a whole were not.

The lesson learned here was to keep property loans completely separated. A bank will attempt to add in other properties as collateral. I would not do it unless you have no other choice and you're looking to purchase a great deal.

As the deal continued to progress toward bankruptcy, I contacted the lender to let them know I was interested in purchasing the property when it was foreclosed. I heard nothing for two more months, and then one day in December 2010 I received a call from a real estate broker who was representing the bank. This call pertained to this Mt. Dora property.

He said, "I heard through the grapevine you want to purchase the strip center."

I replied, "You heard correct."

His next question was, "What price do you want to pay?"

The thought that quickly ran through my head was that I wanted to pay as low a price as possible but not get ridiculous with the offer and lose the deal.

I was thinking about an offer of $275,000 but blurted out, "How about $250,000?"

The broker said that was about the price he was thinking. We ended up agreeing to a price of $255,000, and the bank also replaced the septic system and paid $10,000 to replace some rotten wood and replace a broken a/c system.

So, I would have paid $500,000 for this property three years earlier but was able to purchase it for $255,000. Back in 2007 the owner wanted to sell and retire. He should have been realistic and sold it for the real market value instead of some dream price that never happened. If you really want or need to sell your property, be realistic on the price. If it has not sold in six weeks, you are asking too much or maybe you need to do some maintenance.

Six months after purchasing the property I decided to take out a loan on the property. Why would I do this if the property was purchased with cash? I did a new loan for $200,000 to free up equity to purchase a new property when a good deal comes along. I now own a property with only $55,000 of my own money in the deal. Let's take a financial look at this deal.

Purchase price	$ 255,000.00
new loan	$ 200,000.00
amount invested	$ 55,000.00

Gross income (yearly)	$ 48,000.00

Expenses

Loan pmt	$ 18,000.00
property taxes	$ 4,000.00
property insurance	$ 1,700.00
electric	$ 1,600.00
water treatment	$ 1,560.00
garbage pickup	$ 1,764.00
landscaping	$ 2,100.00
Total	$ 30,724.00

Net Income	$ 17,276.00

Return on Investment (17276/55000)= 31% return on money

Also, the debt on the loan is being paid down. I am gaining a good tax deduction because the IRS allows you to depreciate the property.

TAKE AWAY: Knowledge of the market and patience allowed me the opportunity to purchase property below market value.

TRAITS: Perseverance and Determination
Communication Skills
Passion
Knowledge of Industry

Clermont Property

Recently I was working on purchasing a 17,000 square foot property in Clermont, FL. It is a retail strip center that was built in 1990. The property was for sale five years ago for $1.2 million. One year ago it was listed for sale again at $825,000 on a short sale. It is a short sale because the owner owes more than the property is worth. I contacted the real estate agent to gather information on the property. After my evaluation I told the realtor the property was worth about $560,000, in my opinion. The realtor said the owner would not go lower than $825,000 on the price. I thanked the realtor for her time and told her when the price gets to the $500,000 range to give me a call back.

One year later I received a call saying they had just reduced the price to $550,000. I verified that all of the same tenants were still leasing at the property even though it was only 50% leased out. We wrote up the contract for $550,000. The owner owed about $1 million on the property. Then we waited; we could not move forward with due diligence until the bank accepted our offer which was a lot less than the note on the property. The process of the bank accepting our offer or even responding can take several months. It only took two weeks in this case, and the bank surprisingly accepted our offer without even making a counter offer.

Our 30 day due diligence began. The inspection, survey, and appraisal went well. It was about five days before the due diligence was over. This was where I played some poker and tried to get a better deal. I started getting a vibe from the realtor that the lender really wanted to unload this property and was willing to negotiate further. So why not try to get a better deal? I had nothing to lose. If the bank denied my request I was still going forward with the deal. The bank did not know that though. I had to be careful with the words I used because I did not want to say "if my demands are not met I am cancelling the contract". However, I wanted to be firm enough with the lender so they knew I was serious with my request and may walk away from the deal (even though I was definitely purchasing). Here is the exact email I sent to the realtor:

> "Hi Sue, after inspecting the property, including the roof, it is going to take 40k for me to bring the property up to an acceptable level. Please notify the lender of my request of 40k to be paid to me at closing. If you can find out from the lender if this is acceptable by Thursday (3 days from now) that would be great since I have 2 other properties in the Orlando area that I am interested in pursuing if the bank cannot agree to the 40k. If this is acceptable to the bank I can close in 2 weeks from today."

To my shock, two days later the bank agreed to pay my $40,000 at closing. Little did they know that I was bluffing about cancelling the contract and was still going to purchase the property with or without the $40,000. I would say this was a pretty good hand of poker.

During this same time, the bank I was getting a loan from had guaranteed a loan with the terms of 29% down and 15 years amortization. I wanted a loan with 25% down and 20 year amortization to keep my monthly payments as low as possible. After the appraisal came in $100,000 higher than the sales price of the property, the lender allowed me to put 25% down but still insisted on the 15 year amortization. What could I do now? It seemed as though I was going to have to accept the 15 year amortization.

After some further thought, I offered to put $30,000 in a checking account at the bank if they would agree to the 20 year amortization. The $30,000 could only be used for improvements to the property. I was planning on spending $30,000 on the property during the first month anyway. By thinking outside the box I was able to think of a way to talk the bank into agreeing to the 20 year amortization.

TAKE AWAY: Again, knowledge of the market allowed me to purchase below market value.

TRAITS: Perseverance and Determination
Communication Skills
Passion
Knowledge of Industry

How to Build a Putter

Growing up, golf was my game and a big part of my life. For years I played golf every day, and golf was pretty much all that was on my mind. I became a pretty good golfer except for one thing. I could never quite master the art of putting. Eventually, I realized that my ambition of being a scratch or professional golfer was not going to happen due to my poor putting abilities. The irony of golf is that a two-foot putt counts the same as a 300-yard drive. Back in the 1930's Gene Sarazen made an attempt to have golf move to a larger golf hole so the importance of putting was not so great. Unfortunately, this failed to catch on.

I recently started thinking there had to be a better way to putt, rather than the traditional way. The two basic ways to putt are either the open close method or square to square. I always felt I could not keep my hands steady enough; I think they call that the yips. A couple of years ago I started putting off of the toe of the putter. Unorthodox yes, but it was effective for me. I then thought that if this helped me perhaps I could help others putt better. Most people at this point would say, "I can't make a putter", and that would be the end of it. But that does not work for me.

Even though I know nothing about designing a putter, I pushed forward. I emailed all of my friends to see if anyone could draw designs for a putter. One of my friends is an engineer and said he could help. I told him to draw up designs similar to the putter I was currently using. He drew up the designs. I then set out to find a machine shop that could take the drawings and turn them into reality. Finally I found a local machine shop with which I could work. I thought they would treat me fairly.

At the first meeting with the people at the machine shop I was told that the drawing was not adequate. I had to get some better drawings. My friend could not help me anymore on the drawings at this time. I did not want to hire a company to do the drawings for two reasons. First of all, this would get expensive, and secondly, I still did not know what the final design was going to look like. The design was a work in progress. So I opened my desk drawer, pulled out a pen and ruler and drew up my own designs.

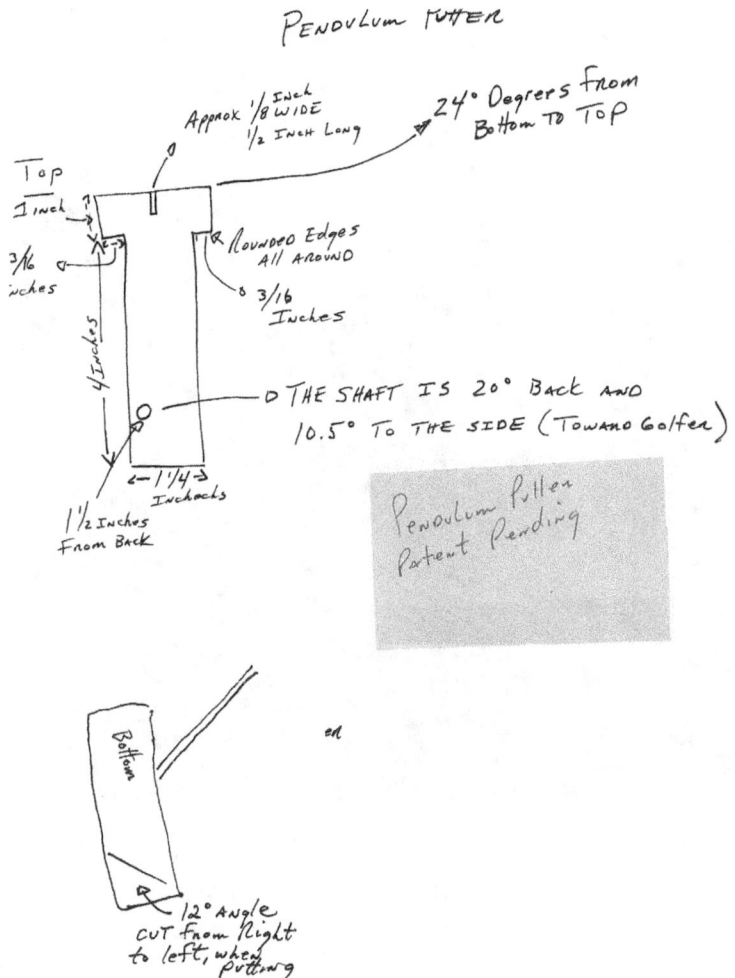

I took the designs to the machine shop, and they made the first putter pictured below.

The first putter ended up feeling too light and did not seem to have enough integrity or stability as it hit the golf ball. Therefore, I found a company in Georgia that sold 50 and 100 gram stainless steel weights. I put two 50 gram weights in the front and one 100 gram weight toward the back of the putter. This took care of the weight and stability problem. The putter now tended to stay in line and not twist as the golf ball was hit.

Here is the updated model:

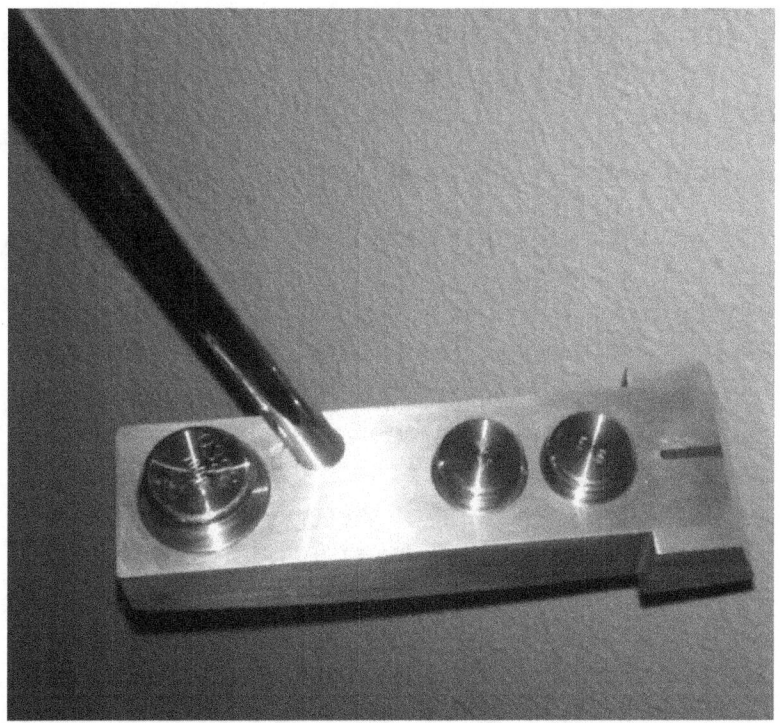

At the present time I use the putter when I golf but have not sold any yet. I am currently working on a marketing campaign. I think I will call this business Erwin Golf, Inc.

Summary

God wants you to be successful-

We have all heard it at our place of worship, the wealthy are tempted by too many of earth's pleasures and will ultimately be sinful. The church preaches that being wealthy is bad. I disagree. God wants you to be successful and to use your talents to the best of your ability. In addition, the wealthy are able to donate more money to churches, charities, and other noble endeavors.

Do not make decisions based on the tax code-

The current Federal tax code is ridiculous. I call it "Government Gone Wild". My accountant recently told me that if I tried my best to follow each rule of the tax code I still would not be able to do it because the code has gotten too confusing and ridiculous. Make investment decisions on the validity of how good the investment is, not on possible tax consequences. If you hold an investment property for longer than one year before selling, you pay a much lower rate of 15% on the income earned. It is not a surprise that the fastest growing regions of the country are in the states with no state income tax.

Massive tax write-off on commercial properties-

I do not pay Federal income tax. There are massive write-offs on commercial property. I have not paid Federal income tax in five years due to the massive tax benefits of owning commercial property. This is definitely a large advantage of owning commercial property. The system of having large tax write-offs for property owners was setup by the Federal government to encourage more investing in property. With the increase in property ownership, it is easier for low income households to find affordable places to live. I wish the Federal Government would switch to a flat tax or fair tax and get rid of all these loopholes even though this loophole benefits me greatly.

Business plans over rated-

Too many unknown variables go into forecasting a business plan. The business plan becomes a guess-timate into future years. I would either recommend passing on the business plan or just putting together some basic thoughts. The most important thing is putting your good idea into action. Get the business going. When I say get the business going, this does not mean you have to quit your job right away or spend a lot of money. For example, I have been working on my golf putter business for about one year and have only spent $1500 so far. Moving forward cautiously is okay. Most people do the "cautious" part but never do the "move forward" part.

Refinance to get cash out-

My normal advice is, don't sell your commercial property investments. If the property was good enough when you purchased it, most likely it is still good enough today. But if the property has increased in value and you want to get the money out of it, what do you do? If you sell the property, you have to pay capital gains taxes and you no longer own the property. What you want to do is refinance the property and pull the money out tax free. You still own the property.

Hewlett Packard 12B (Business Calculator) -

It is imperative that you become familiar with using a business calculator. How are you going to know what your monthly payment will be on a business, property, or car purchase? It is not hard to learn how to use these calculators. The owner's manual is very easy to understand. There are five variables, and you will need information on three of these variables to make a calculation.

The five variables are n (number of years in the loan), I (the interest rate), pv (the amount of the loan), pmt (what the payment is), and fv (what is the future value of the loan). For example, if you have a 20 year loan for $100,000 at 6% interest you can figure out the payment: 20 yrs = n, 100,000=pv, and 6%=i. Then just hit the payment button to get your payment.

Conclusion:

Your passion is everything. Do what you love. Whatever your passion, if you do it better than anyone else you will be rich. I know a person who is passionate about making nuts and bolts. His business has grown very large, and he is quite successful. When I talk with him he talks about nuts and bolts, and I can hear the passion in his voice.

Listen to your inner passion. Believe in yourself because you can do it. I have figured out that writing books is not my passion; it is boring for me. This will probably be my last book, but I wanted to encourage you in your business ventures by sharing some of the things I have learned.

Good luck on your future endeavors. Now get up and do it.